T0287685

the answer to everything

Caitlin Press Inc.
3375 Ponderosa Way
Qualicum Beach, BC V9K 2J8
www.caitlin-press.com

Reprinted with the permission of Harbour Publishing, www.harbourpublishing.com
"Weed book drift," "Land schemas," "Roadkill," "Salmon," "The journeyman," "Forget it" from *Ecologue* by Ken Belford, 2005

Reprinted with the permission of Talonbooks
pages 5, 6, 10, 14, 18, 26, 27, 32-34, 52, 59-61, 72, 73, 81, 83, 85, 91, 92 from *Decompositions* by Ken Belford, 2010

pages 1-3, 13, 16, 21, 22, 31, 32, 35, 39, 44, 47, 54, 56, 60, 65, 67, 68, 69, 77, 78 from *Internodes* by Ken Belford, 2013

pages 3, 5-9, 12, 15-16, 19-21, 30-31, 44-47, 51-52, 62-65, 70-71, 86 from *Slick Reckoning* by Ken Belford, 2016

Text and cover design by Vici Johnstone. Cover image by Si Transken

Printed in Canada

Caitlin Press Inc. acknowledges financial support from the Government of Canada and the Canada Council for the Arts, and the Province of British Columbia through the British Columbia Arts Council and the Book Publisher's Tax Credit.

Library and Archives Canada Cataloguing in Publication

The answer to everything : selected poems of Ken Belford / edited by Jordan Scott, Rob Budde & Si Transken.

Poems. Selections
Belford, Ken, 1946-2020 author. | Scott, Jordan, 1978- editor. | Budde, Robert, 1966- editor. | Transken, Si, 1960- editor.

Canadiana 20210198516 | ISBN 9781773860688 (softcover)
LCC PS8503.E47 A6 2021 | DDC C811/.54—dc23

the answer to everything

SELECTED POETRY OF KEN BELFORD

Edited by Rob Budde & Si Transken,
Consulting Editor Jordan Scott

CAITLIN PRESS 2021

Contents

FOREWORD
by Rob Budde

> I remembered the answer to everything—
> there's always something wrong
> with everything.
>
> Ken Belford, 2019

"The answer to everything" is Ken Belford's last poem, written a few months before he died February 19, 2020. It was written through the pain and exhaustion cancer imposes on the body, but it is written with determination, clarity, and generosity—all the elements of Belford's indominable spirit.

There are many elements that distinguish Ken's poetry in Canadian poetics; I will discuss very little of them here because I want to spend more time talking about his private process and worldview. He established a distinct assemblage poetics based on semantic slippage and disjunctive other-than-lyric 'gaps.' His 'lan(d)guage' is like nothing else; he tied the rhythms and codes of poetry to the natural dynamics of the unroaded mountain country, from the perspective of out there, looking back at the cities from the forest, from Blackwater Lake (T'amtuuts'whl'ax, north of Hazelton in the Skeena Mountains). His poetry asserted an outside, an other, in two ways: a cultural distance gained from 30 years as a back-country guide trained by Gitxsan hereditary chiefs (foremost being Walter Blackwater) and in terms of gender expression, openly resisting the sexist 'paternal' and misogynist 'poetry boy gangs'. It was an ethics we shared as close friends and structured our stand in Prince George/Lheidli T'enneh Territory against the status quo.

Ken's ethics, his anti-racism (borne out of the treaty process), his feminism (informed in part by his partner Si Transken), and his resistance to more conventional poetics modes, all contributed to his remote place in the poetic landscape. I hope this book, selected with his input and edited by those who knew and respected him, is chosen by future scholars as a representative introduction to his work.

This introduction will be careful, kind, and personal, much the same tone an afternoon conversation with Ken over coffee would be. For those who visited Prince George and experienced Ken's hospitality, I want you to recognize his calm gentleness and generosity. For those who have not met him, I want to channel my inner Ken—all the balanced ways of being he gave to me in our many years of friendship—to provide a context for the poems in this collection.

Ken often spoke of his 'other lives'—specifically two other lives: one in

Vancouver as a young man and one on Blackwater Lake. His third life was here in Prince George where he lived on Central Street and then Spruce Street from 2004 until 2020 with poet/activist/social worker/professor Dr. Si Transken.

West End Vancouver in the 1960s was where Ken first started writing—this was the era of TISH, founded by such poets as George Bowering, Fred Wah, Frank Davey, Daphne Marlatt, David Cull, Carol Bolt, Dan McLeod, Robert Hogg, Jamie Reid, and Lionel Kearns. Ken sat in on poetry classes at UBC and SFU—not as a registered student (he had a Grade 10 education at the time) but, even then, as an independent scholar, a liminal presence, an outsider. In conversations with me, he identified as, not 'anti-TISH', but 'other-than-TISH'. "Ken was one of the old-style, self-taught poets like Al Purdy, Patrick Lane and John Newlove who forged his art outside the academy and drew on the experience of work and the life of the street for his inspiration," says Howard White, who published Belford's fifth poetry book, *ecologue* (Harbour, 2005). As you will see in this collection of his work, Ken's poetry transformed from the poetics of those self-taught poets into something different, something I don't think compares easily to anything else in Canadian poetics.

Drawn by work and something else ("fate or dissatisfaction?" Ken once ruminated), Ken went North. Some fruit picking in the Okanagan but mostly North North, for a time working in a printshop in the basement of what is now Books & Company on 3rd Avenue in Prince George. Perhaps more importantly Ken worked in the Smithers/Hazelton area cutting cedar shakes. It was at this time that he felt the pull of the mountains and the green valleys north of roads and north of convention. He spent time with Patrick Lane, on worksites and out hunting, which produced the iconic cover photo of *Post Electric Caveman*. Worked at other odd jobs, though Ken often said he has never worked a day in his life, which I always interpreted as he always did things he loved and/ or never felt beholden to a boss. A good state to be in when writing.

After some years farming near Seeley Lake just West of Hazelton—a beautiful place Ken and I visited on a road trip back to that area—and meeting his first partner Alice, Ken went deeper, further into the mountains, buying the rights to guide on the territory around what is known on most maps as Blackwater Lake. This is Gitxsan territory and accessible only by float plane and walking in. And this is where Ken learned the old names (T'amtuuts'whl'ax) and developed deep relationships with chiefs (Walter Blackwater and Neil Sterritt most notably). With Alice and their new daughter Hannah, Ken hosted wealthy American democrats to experience the lake, rivers, and forest. At first it was fly-in fishing expeditions but then Ken transitioned to a form of ecotourism (before the word existed) that was low impact and did not kill fish or animals. He became a vegetarian at this time and, as he would say, would eat "nothing with a face."

I first contacted Ken Belford in 2004, on the advice of Barry McKinnon, who had known him for many years and helped him publish *Pathways into the Mountains* in 2000. I heard he was knowledgeable about fish and I had a question about Steelhead Trout. So, I emailed him and soon received a reply in the form of a 3-page love letter to Steelhead Trout. I was wondering if it was salmon or like the Lake Trout I knew from time in Yellowknife NWT. Instead I got a detailed description of the personality, family structure, and movements of the fish. He wrote about how returning Steelhead recognized him, as they looked up from a pool that they returned to year after year. This careful attention and genuine love for the life of all creatures is what I would want you to know most about the Ken Belford I know. The image of him quietly standing by a river eddy, greeting the Steelhead individuals and families, is something I will carry with me forever.

Ken spoke about how this time—time cutting trails, standing in the river, carving tool handles, interacting with the animals, the forest, the weather—changed him. That much time outside the cities, towns, rural, roaded and human-influenced places, changed his view *looking back at them*—back to the polluting cattle farms, back to the consumptive cities, from the mountains, from the edge of the forest. This specific form of biofilia is an element hinted at in his early writing but fully realized in his later books. The land knowledge, the 'lan(d)guage' Ken deploys is based on those 30 years walking the forest, encountering the animals, navigating the water, and relating to the ecosystems. This knowledge was a blend of book knowledge and lived knowledge, and came to be in stark contrast to the representation of "nature" in Canadian lyric poetry. The 'lived' knowledge was not just being there and seeing things, but in practice and building knowledge—a relationship with the land—over time. He spoke often of learning, after much practice and experimentation, how to walk best hip deep in various kinds of river currents. He spoke of recognizing how the lake would 'flip' its waters at a certain time of year and certain temperature. He spoke of learning to hear moose calls up and down the valley in the evening, if one sat very still, and how to recognize the very loose wide-ranging 'herds' that they created.

He compared working on editing poems to making tools—and he made many, often carving handles and even engine parts from wood—until they work right and fit well in your hands. This poem from *Finding Ft. George* was inspired by that discussion, but also an imitation of how Belford often interleaved references to material/natural phenomena and writing:

the slurry

as ideas move across, a wet inter
action will form, made
of material from the sharpening
mind and the listener--it is junk
remains in the poem to facilitate
slippage and friction

as the moisture in the language
drops, it is crucial that it be kept wet,
slurry re-applied to the reading act because
it contains all the particles—the pieces and fragments
shift shift shift of thought up until that point in the
text—and so will sound
out meaning: fine, keen, ready to work
out there

The word "interleaving" is one term I think accurately describes Ken's compositional process; he would often take disparate semantic realms of thought and interweave them throughout a poem or set of poems. This juxtaposition functions not like a metaphor, but created resonances across the locations of thought in more subtle complicated ways. So, one of my reading strategies when spending time with a Belford poem is to open up my reading stance so I am not looking for a single line of argument or location of representation, or even two parallel tracks, but instead I am paying attention to the ways the zones interact, like the complex ecology of a place.

The relationship he built with the physical place of Blackwater Lake was partly guided (the guide being guided) by Gitxsan elders and chiefs. By boat and on the ancient trails still visible in the region, Ken spent time with these holders of knowledge that transcended the colonial books and ways of seeing. I imagine, the elders, chiefs, and other Gitxsan knowledge-holders took Ken into their confidence because of his growing knowledge of the land and the respect he had for it. They gave him hand-drawn maps, showed him traditional sites and CMTs, and walked with him on the ancient trails of the region. Some of this contact and communication came around the deliberations and consultations on the Nisga'a Treaty, which came into effect in 2000. From Ken's account of the treaty process it was incredible complex and divisive. The main role he had, given his knowledge of the region, was to help establish Gitxsan title to lands that the government had mistakenly (or deliberately, in order to create discord) proposed as Nisga'a territory. The process produced three effects on Ken that I could discern: one, a sense of the value of careful and considered negotiation, two, a wary eye to the machinations of affluent white men and, three, a deepening of his respect for Indigenous ways of being and knowing (TEKW). As a white man, Ken knew not to make any claims to this knowledge, knew not to recolonize by taking that knowledge as a possession or accolade, but it did change his world view, and is an indispensable lens when looking at his poetry.

Ken's time at his lodge ended with a divorce with Alice and a move to Smithers and then Prince George. The move into town was a kind of retirement, the physical demands of guiding becoming difficult. It did mean more writing time and closer ties with writing communities. On the positive side this meant more contact with other writers in Prince George. On the negative side this meant more contact with other writers in Prince George. In our correspondence between 2004 and 2010, largely by email and over coffee at Second Cup at 15th and Victoria St. in Prince George, it became increasingly apparent that Ken did not feel he 'fit in' locally. His discomfort came from several aspects: his decision to not drink alcohol, his feminist grounding, and, enveloping all this, his sense that his experiences had led him away from what he saw as generally conservative forms of writing.

So, his relationships switched to stronger and continuing relationships with a wider set of writers: Jordan Scott, Rita Wong, Larissa Lai, Jeff Derksen, Jay MillAr, Jake Kennedy, Reg Johanson, Dorothy Trujillo Lusk, Christine Stewart, and Tsering Wangmo Dhompa, to name a few. He was influenced by political activist work by Carol J. Adams, Harsha Walia, and Vandana Shiva. Well-worn books on his shelf included ones by Frank O'Hara, Adrienne Rich, Charles Bernstein, and Robert Creeley; the later of these he had a long extensive correspondence with and he visited Creeley in Florida in the late 1990s.

I have a record of the many years of correspondence between Ken and myself, emails from 2005—2014. They trail off when we switched to texting. It was an exchange that helped form who I am as a man and thinker and poet, and I owe Ken a debt of gratitude for that. It was primarily a conversation around an ethics we shared all along and helped structure our writing and mentorship of other new writers:

On 10/8/06 11:45 AM, "Ken Belford" <kenbelford@shaw.ca> wrote:

Back when I workt in the treaty process, there came a time when racism and sexism became more than intellectual or political principle but a poison to me, a moment when I consciously moved into the knowing how vile these two human habits are, so when confronted by it since then, I resist it in the now. Like I say, I'm proud of you and your values. I honour our friendship. We are good for each other and our relationship is healthy.

I have many memories: visiting Gitwangak/Kitwanga "Battle Hill," a KSW reading at Coop Books, biking downtown, spending time with Ken and his little cat CB, the trip we took with Si on their honeymoon, stopping by the glaciers on the way to Banff, walks all over town. I feel like Ken and I had more work to do; but I guess that will have to wait for someplace else another time.

On 7/27/06 10:05 PM, "Ken Belford" <kenbelford@shaw.ca> wrote:

I thought of a place where we could share a cabin but we'd have to fly in but it could be set up legally. On Wiminosik Lake ... or on Nass Lake. Wiminosik would be the least vulnerable and a little cheaper to get to. It's probably too far. Wiminosik is a Gtxsan name for a chief, a chief who is a friend. Weee—min ah sick is how you'd say it. Winminosik is not too far from Blackwater. Really wild. Grizzly country. Many little rainbows. Great wild berry picking, especially Raspberry. It's the wildness though. Good drinking water too. Well, at least now you know one place is there. I'm not sure I'd want to start all over with building again but maybe. The place exists. In this conversation, one would have to license it under my old guide license, otherwise, there's no way. It's a thought, a lovely thought. Maybe best kept that way. In my mind I see it.

Okay Ken. Meet you there.

The Legend of Ken

If that is his name, walking away
from the main, from the culture of knowledge
and response, if that is his body there
leaning into the currents just this much, just
enough to step ahead of the force, talking
to the steelhead, making language old again;
if those are his words flowing around
each other and making the animals tracks and fish
paths in the development slough;
if that is Ken then I am his friend,

11

following his rhythms of letting go,
of leaving behind the poet voice, of foregoing
the kill shot, of side-stepping the place affiliations
that erase, that cede, that road over something other;
if that is Ken then let this be the offering,
the sharing over a hearth, the saying of the names.

In my view, Ken hit the pinnacle of his poetic abilities in his last four books. He admitted to me he was a little embarrassed by some of the pieces in his early books. 'Another life' he would say. The final years of Ken's life was, I think, another life too; it was a time of pain and struggle as cancer came and went through his body. But it was also the time he wrote through the pain to produce *Slick Reckoning*, his last book. My last meetings with Ken were at his townhouse on Spruce Street where Si had planted and developed an amazing garden for birds and stray cats to take refuge in. We met there because he felt nervous about venturing out and not having the energy to make it back home. So, with seven cats lounging and participating, we spent his last months discussing this book, what poems to take from the early books, a few edits and tweaks there, the balance of pages across the books, what themes to pull forward in the selections, what publishers might be interested, and who might help with an introduction. It was only a few weeks after we had finished that process that he had a fall and could not recover.

Well over a year later I am still coming to terms with this loss.

Working on this book has helped; it is an odd mix of celebration and mourning. I am grateful for the loving work of Si Transken, Jordan Scott, Sarah Corsie, and Vici Johnstone in bringing this book together.

I think this selection will give the reader an accurate sense of how the early books informed the later, how the themes of environmental awareness, his alienation, and his sense of social justice developed over the years. I also think it will be a suitable monument to a monumental man, my best friend forever, Ken Belford.

On the Other Path

The other day I saw your
swerve in the way saplings bent
around the day, and the loons
and petrol still fight it out on
the way to the store. Snags
of logs in the way I write now
and the roll is everything.

Maybe that's all there is:
a reshaping of the forest
as you pass, heavy-footed or
speaking the tongue of sphagnum
fluent, like you actually care,
a nudge in pronunciation as
you pass by a breeze of text
intent on nothing
and everything stirs
an answer.

Rob Budde

FIREWEED (1967)

To the Reader

This is a different sky.
If I close my hand
I hold the knife.

Do not let me live.
Do not let me love.
Then see what I mean.

I am the knife.
I cut.
Keep me nervous.

Or, as I said once,
It's the war of the wild shot,
In a poem I gave away.

Premise for Fireweed

i
Ageless, in a magenta chalice,
Keen as blood, a man in me is hanging,
Inverted.

A man with his back to
A garden of fireweed turns in me.
Consummate so. And deflecting.

ii
He's been there since
The season under way.

Since the weeds came.
So many, and thick,
While trying to weed them out,
The flowers came too.

A small world of damp things
Meant to be beautiful.
And dangling from my hand.

iii
There is no choice.
I speak of the later fireweed.
The season under way.

I speak of weeds. Of fire.
For, as I've learned, fire can teach you,
If you go naked.

iv
Seasonless now, he endures
This side of winter.
Changeless.

And I am the one being weathered.
It accounts for the bur
On my pantleg.

The Wolf Path

It's not the dog at the end of the chain.
Dream running on the wolf path.
Trailing familiars in his sadder dream.

That dream is mine.
How the chain is always tight.
These are things I know: I accept.

And it's not the winter hanging on.
Until finally all things
Are beginning to die.

But it's the way the place shifts,
Inching now and then toward the river bank
Makes the wolves turn and me wonder.

Turn (a poem in 4 parts)

i
What they are doing is turning
The earth
In ordered furrows.

Where it is blackest and most fit.
Laying muscles of earth
One beside the other.

And tomorrow, they will return
To harvest the rocks.
Rocks that are drawn from a deeper seeding.

That come with the same energy
That allows the willow to spring straight.
It comes thru, as elsewhere.

ii
Familiar comes the carrion odour of earth.
Douglas, I said, what do you think of all day?
Nothing, he replied. Nothing.

Which is difficult to understand,
Considering I have watched them all day
From a larger expanse of rock.

iii
Groaning, the stoneboat
Skids, lurches, approaches,
Draws nearer the edge.

Animals break
With the sound,
Bursting across the clearing.

Nothing, he said. The air smells sweet of death.
Of earth, of flowers. Nothing is impossible.
Gee up, he calls to his horse, following.

iv
The one furrow doesn't turn with the others,
Leads off into the brush. The man is gone
But the boot prints remain. He will never come
        back.

First Wild Wolves

I have been dying all day.
First wild wolves came down from the
       mountains,
Killed a moose on the river ice.

One cut it down from behind.
The other bled it.
First the worm comes. Then the bird.

Watched from the window.
Knowing of and fearing more than
One kind of death.

An ice octopus drapes one more arm downward.
I can't get used to the room.
The furniture doesn't fit somehow.

Erasure

i
It is hard to tell how far away
The mountains really are. They seem closer,
But they must be fifteen miles, maybe more.

And what is between is like an August haze.
Only it is not. It is February and cold.
My eyes travelling to that edge again.

To what is a thickening mist.
Both sheltering and raging
Against what I can half see.

ii
I know how thin the crust is in parts.
I know that mist as fear. Behind it is the avalanche
My poems are small cries: nothing more.

Black Lake, #1

I am becoming aware
Of a real boat
In the back water of me.

Two men in it cast their lines,
But the green living things have gone
Because the lake is dead.

Dusk

From an old man
In an Autumn garden,
I learned how to get all the vegetables in.

Look again.
It is not a blue sky or coloured like the sea.
It is of things much darker.

It is an anguished sky
That passes over the moon
And it makes me nervous.

He is still alive I hear.
Cutting brush every day
And folding his clothes carefully.

Absorption

The description of the landscape doesn't matter.
What matters is
That the door has been left ajar.

That I will disappear here
Into the brush,
And will reappear at the other side.

Carrier

They have no word for conscience.
Instead, say *sdzî*, meaning
Heart.

Practical people who associate words differently.
For example, marriage, say *me—at*, sex. Legend has it
When someone you have loved dies, part of your heart dies too.

They burnt the body. Not cremated. Burnt.
From then, to carry the basket of ash. To continue.
To hunt. To trap. *Alkoh tsûtgen*, let us sing together.

To bear the ashes until a future final marriage.
A band of thieves, and liars.
Stunted, inter-related.

People with large eyes.
Having nowhere to go:
I am one of them.

THE POST ELECTRIC CAVE MAN (1970)

Poets, Children, Pensioners

We didn't know what we were holding—
          it was heavy, energy; the
     wheels went
               round and round for
     no reason.
               Hammers, bells, and copper;
          we thought it was fun.
                    Joking, she said
          I shouldn't take it
                    so seriously. Tissue
     poems,
     warm children, poets, pensioners
                    and scars:
          all the world is flesh. The
          displacement has been noticed.

               Outpost
     in the city? Anyway, set back
               from the others.
With two addresses.

The view spins
               in the tree, in
                    the circular tree. Fences
          are grown over, and things have been
     let
          go.

     Silently, and second from the last, the
          tall gray weeds
choke themselves.
                    And there is no back yard, no
          alley, but
                    the door to it is
          open.

For Kelley

Take a look, i
sd, i sat
there

singing, dumb-
ly, as all
things

do, alone.
And i sat there
as long as

you, a sound
became
a breath

to me, saying
the same
dumb

sound
over and
over

The In-Between

And though I've since forgotten
                the in-between
       this is what I can remember:
                        that I was raised
                    in a small prairie building
          pierced the sky's belly. Nights
    there were fireflies in the wind:
                        my uncle
                        leaning into the flashlight
          saying
                    "you know I can walk on water." Other nights
                        a tightening stillness
            and a local humming of space
                        and I screaming.
            And my younger brother laughing endlessly
                    below me.
                            And
                I can remember my father
       remember him
                        now
                    as he turned
            down the road toward us one day in winter—
                        watching him as he grew
                    larger
                    until when he passed the window
       his face was splotched purple from a disease
there is no name to;
                    that his skin was stretched tight
            and no features showed.

"The People, Yes, The People"
—Carl Sandburg

In the year of the
famine, the year the
caterpillars came,
when the people
were starving, when

they admitted
to themselves
they had nothing, it was then
they found that, together
thru the need to visit, and to
speak

that
altho it was true
each of them had
little to offer, as
men, that,
out of need,

when they gathered,
there were enough
holy grains to
weather the season
of drought, of loneliness, of
doubt; the present one.

2

In spots
it is warm enough
and in those spots
it is a good knot I tie.
Otherwise, it is winter.

And, in winter,
it is always one day from spring.

It is always a false thaw.

On the river
ice to the horses
I am
with my bucket
of oats.
There are no gardeners
in the forest
and these are not
the only tracks
I discover.

So I lay my ear
down along the cold
steel rail to hear
something of her passage:
there was nothing.

Branches Back Into

His job was
to walk in
front of me, I can
remember the sharp swing

of the wet swollen
branches back into
my face, feel it now,
now as the
skin rises,

can feel the
sudden white lines
they made on my skin, as
I followed him, holding
my end of the chain

in the one hand, in
the other, a
small axe for
notching
the trees. No

one has since
followed us, or
built the road
it was to
be, be. I

can remember
falling, waste deep
in muskeg water, remember
only the outline
of his back

ahead of me, not
seeing the mountains
we were in: they
were unimaginable,
exceed me.

Remember few words
passed between us, he
ahead of me
with his instruments
recording it all,

can remember, too, how
I answered him,
never once faltering,
shouting, even
though long

ago I had lost
my axe and was
too afraid
to tell him.

Origins

Inside
my solitude, either
in wilderness
or in the city, in

my vigil, most
everything
has fallen or
warped or turned

to rust. Cars,
origins, alphabets,
indifference—
I have seen

a clotted dream turning, turn
to slow bars of
pure colour. Below
this,

this building, I
am living, in solitude,
in a house with no sound,
with a woman

who is my wife, partly. I
have learned
to control
nothing.

Level

This is for you.
No one else
will ever have
a copy of this.

I've got two
hours to go
till I hit
prince george

and you'll
be still
not there,
in that city

either.

In Solitude, I

Returning, but to a
different kind of solitude,
I remember when I was
in wilderness, I
put out the sound of the

paper, the poem
on it, refused it,
stapled it flat
on the door
in the wind

as opposed to
the sound of the
chimes. And realized later,
when it was too late
they were the same.

Not only
had you written
with your right, but
with your left
hand, as

it opened, had
given me sound for the
emptiness carved by the
right, which is what you
said, and what you wrote.

PATHWAYS INTO THE MOUNTAINS (2000)

Sign Language (3)

Beams around me, a
washing machine, a
window to measure
the passage of sun, overhead.
slits, in the window, for air.

downstairs is bottom,
flat bottom, a place
to be, where the sewers are,
to carry the rain
away.

I put my ear to the drain,
water enters the house, hundreds
of miles away, men
begin to flood another valley,
Alice brushes her teeth,

water leaves the house. I ask her
what it was she said
made me sit upright
a few days ago, down
stairs, in the bed.
she cannot remember.

only enough light enters
to keep from stumbling,
enough to see outlines, of
her back, the bed, books,
on the table, beside the bed.

downstairs there are no
colours, there we live
in black, black, and white, white.
it is a poor photograph
we have made of ourselves,

and we should have moved,
we should move.

I go back down
stairs, full of bacon,
eggs, honey, and tea.

the taps open and close
beneath her hands, her rings
scrape across the metal,
click, across the dishes,
the water flows

between the walls, past
my ears, through
my throat. the water
is clogged in parts,
in others, clotted with air.

The cat gags on the meat,
coughs it up again, startles me
with her convulsions.
the door is opened, the cat is
put outside.

the dog begins to eat
what the cat couldn't, everywhere
there are teeth, teeth and
spoons.

in my sleeplessness,
the boards become a wall,
air is forced, in pipes, across
and below the floors,
more oil burns,
the valley floods, trees are
flattened

into boards, the lights
go on, the earth turns
our of darkness, lights
in the windows, across my face,
the pupils shrink,
my eyes become slits.

Sign Language (14)

I come to the meeting,
late
   when
they are cleaning up.
I had wanted
      to the tune
      of rain
no better weather
to do it in.
And I had wanted something
not so unlike bark
from all the battles
from the bottom
of the spine, up.

One works alone in the shed
when the wrenches spread.

Break any bone you want
but break the back
and no more fight: this
side of the building is white.

I come late to the meeting
in time
      to wonder
who came,
      who left
and who spoke.

And I among things
that distress children
wanted to know
if he spoke at all.
      And
if he did
easily.

Holding Land

The return: everything was as we left it,
mild winter, no predation
yet. The water I mean
some never drank.

Small and abundant valley,
we saw the timbers out
and pack them in, lumber
piling up, roughcut
Spruce and Balsam on our backs,
uphill, on the way in.

Always I have been afraid
of this moment:
breaking the land.

O well we say
let the damn wind blow.
Well, I hope it will
bring something in
and there we will go
again, as when packing out,
with it, one step at a time.

Rewriting

If down the logging road
the carcasses go
just before dark,
what man-eating beast of prey
prowls after this?

Blood, flesh and horn by dark
but at arrival of new day,
first glance of seedbed, bud and gem,
source re-opening.

Starting over, thinking twice,
writing and rewriting
this devegetizing kind of industry
harms land so it suffers and aches.
It's no wonder
they throw their money away
while ranging the streets afterward
with a hardon and a pocket full of money,
they know it's no good.
It's profit but it isn't generous,
desirable but not conscientious
and the bland are fickle.

But you have to believe in something
so I'll believe the time,
the same as yours,
the speed of thought.

Oblique pitch or pulse, beat
outside my window. Reasons, grounds,
calving or spawning pull and push
of sexy lodestar,
irresistible habit forming sorceress
I feel the urge and heal the shot.

A Loss and A Classical Ship

A classical ship sails tonight
full of goons drinking beer

the time could be anytime
today or tomorrow

they don't give anything
all they do is take
these men around here

whenever they kill
whatever they can
they hunger for home

this is the song of the loss
of the land

so busted and open
no cover no more

bulldozers cresting the hill
nothing's too high
nowhere too far

rootsmell on the wind
cedars sold for dope

so overloaded with shit
the river going by
is deformed and undone
but going by anyway
right to the end

as mortise unto tenon
never you undo these bodies

or inhabit our hearts
with your loud motors

For Jack Spicer, Now

A poem cannot be as pure
as a seagull's belly.

Those who ask this of poetry
cannot fish without bait
or think carrying pencils into wilderness
brings words back out.

Stolen words are never pure,
liver flukes in the belly.

The Consumption of the Nass

It's morning and no one else is up.
Another night of rain, away
in the distance the *tak tak tak*
of the Sapsucker killing trees.
Otherwise, silence for the moment.
Even earlier something bigger
went through, not sure what.

I live in a territory
operations men think remote
when it's just pristine.
Natural land is clean land, it's why
it seems so far away, why
the original virtue of unexhausted land
is spoiled by men who
cannot keep their hands off.

Now they begin, the tongues, the
Tanager and Warbler, Blue Bird
and Thrush. Now they find their voices,
an occasion for missing souls
to sympathize.

In my lifetime I will
see this valley go
from spirited wildland
to a devegetized slope.

This is the valley where
no one cares. It is the other place,
the place white men don't live,
the valley where the burglars go.

When I'm gone
the next guy
will be selling tires, gasoline,
roadside coffee and live bait.

Ecologue (2005)

Weed book drift

Loggers wipe their asses with owls,
a synonym for the old growth.
But shit doesn't stick to feathers and
diversity is a moral responsibility
having to do with the transfer of properties.
Economists that neglect problems
choose ignorance and inaction.

Identity, by pointing on a map,
may be inaccurate.
We don't know much.
If we did we'd spend more
on replacing living things
than on building.

The process of temporary states,
including synonyms
for the elk of poetry
spreads like a Bitterroot Cascade
and is called invasion.

Invaders suck up more water,
transform and degrade community
and dirty vehicles spread
the order of magnitude.

By the number of appearances
on weedy lists, testing branches
name stabilized economic plants
and the present system spreads
on a continental scale.

Land schemas

The north moves north.
This song is an article of evidence.
Myths sustain the agenda,
        donuts are the fuel of ragers
        and fantasy is the glue.

        There's grime in the streets
                and I want to know how
                they got the dirt on me.

Most leaves don't touch
        but some appear to like it.
Power is against the good
        and I am a variant
                caught in a contradiction,
                modelled by another, needing to separate
        and grow distinct, to give up
        and go back to the bush
        where love's spongy congress gathers cause.

At first glance into the heavens,
I saw an unlikely elemental ancestry
        set in motion. The head and shoulders
        of a faceless charioteer drawn by stallion.

Who else but Pegasus could this be?
        So that I, the animal's husband
        would then know
        the stem of such descent?

My father farmed, his brothers too, his fathers too.
His hands husked chaff, instinctively he
        disliked weeds and this bad blood
        he saw was not his type and suddenly
                he was out of love for me.

There were fireflies in the pasture
        in the night and against the moon,
                multitudes of breeding and broody birds.

The confide in the earth is to bury,
    to whisper and shade,
    to hide in and cover with dirt.

Vessels are made of soil, mold, dust and clay.
Away in the burrow out of earshot,
    the earthworm snuffles toward connexion,
        an intentional conductor
        zeroing in on the return path.

Roadkill

Snakes bask in the middle,
birds eat the gravel,
mammals eat the salt,
deer eat the brush,
rodents live in the grasses,
songbirds bathe in the dirt,
moose travel along roads
and the scavengers get smacked
right in the centre.
Fragments are islands of trees
between clear-cuts.
These roads suck blood.
The better the highway
the worse it gets.

Salmon

Nearby and side by side,
they are not connected to you.
They are individuals, singular creatures,
earthlings like you.
Don't hound them with hooks,
pester or molest them.
Some are late and some are early.
Some are extinct and the rest are old.
They pour out of the ocean.
You can't send them back.
Believe in them.
Don't exaggerate their size or invest in them.
Forget reliance. All you can do is guess.
Don't agonize over them
when they beat their brains out.
You will put them off with your words.
They have no opinions or answers
and don't belong to you. They long for the depths.
Stubborn and irritable, they have no appetite or thirst.
They have faces and wear stripes.
The dogma of ascent means nothing.
Don't throw dirt on them.
Under the sun, in this world,
they stand on the bottom.

The journeyman

I'm a working class poet, a child of farmers.
I worked in the mills and sorted lumber.
I never taught school and I'm not celebrated.
Can't change that and can't change this.
There wasn't money to send me to school.
I know how to put up hay by hand, how to
make my handles, how to sharpen and
shape, how to join timbers. I lived where
scholars didn't. Little is known of me. Only a
few are like me. I'm Canadian and the
author of these poems. I'm not invited to
read in the universities. They don't know
who I am. I learned to write in the middle
of the night after work was done. I'm thankful
we didn't have a bible. Nothing to read but
I knew I was a poet. None of us were
merchants, none studied the law, none the
healing arts. My father wanted to write. He
sold the farm and we moved to the city.
I found poetry there but I don't know how I
found it. I'll never be a sucky white boy.
I was 58 or 59 when I wrote this in 1741.
There were times I had no store food so I
lived from the land. I'm an unregulated voice
from the Nass. Alfred Purdy noticed me. I'm
ingenuous, have genius and I don't sing when
the harp comes around. Remember my name.
No one protects me. I owned my own boat
and made my own home. That's why poetry.

Forget it

I made my home in another age, dreaming a habitat without a frame. Some people thought it was worthless because it didn't cost much but it took everything I had. I'm still a housekeeper and I don't want to get paid for it. Even back then I didn't do what I was told.

I learned to sharpen anything made to cut. The rest I made smooth. Out of the recurring old growth I ripped all the timbers, planks, shakes and boards I needed, accommodating the checks and rot in the great trees I lived in the shade of. I kept and caught no animals, made an income of my own and grew a few things.

I'm the voice from below. I pity the rich because they have so little. I'm not a socialist and don't own a condo or even a car. I don't see wealth and poverty the way academics do. I didn't ask for money, lived a good life and sacked a few delusions. In the south they are poor. I had land and didn't depend on money or an education, not even status and prestige. Didn't have agents and stood on my own feet. It's not natural to consume so much. What was good for me would be good for you. When I'm angry I imagine hunting trucks, the high ones with horns on their hoods. I live in another economy and it is both older and younger. My money isn't dead. I don't devalue my work. Forget it. I'm not interested in catching up.

LAN(D)GUAGE (2008)

In the presence of blood and lymph, animals forgive
more quickly than men and live next to us
above the level of the sea. Fish browse
in pastures. The fielder returns the ball in play.
Next could be someone else,
the queen of horses, anyone else, a hayfoot
or a strawfoot, a pair of polymorphic likenesses
with short necks and wings.
And there are traps. Those who must have animals
are easily startled or hurt by too much mother
or too much father. The journey
of young men can end in a different place,
where their minds thicken and harden.
The largest predators are never seen.
These are the types: Those who must have animals
with them, those who lie back of form, those
who bring instructions and supplies,
those who are a type of something
and independent of other kinds,
illusionists who say they make reality
and those who tried.

I slept beside a grizzly, each of us unaware
of the other, and when I awakened, heard
his breath next to mine. Time began for me
in that instant when I arose and saw him
sleeping there with a salmonberry leaf
on his head. No longer alone, all things since
are altered by that switch. What else is there
to know, each of us asleep and happy?
But he awakened just then and barreled off
into the brush, toward everything necessary.
At that moment everything I knew left me
and now a new world has taken place.
It comes to the same thing—astonishment
that this should happen at all. But I heard
him breathe, and saw him make tracks
before I could think. To see this thing
was not horrendous, and to see it go
was not delightful. Nothing meaningful
occurred, but time started with a big bear.
This is not about anything, but I'm waiting
for some thing to come up behind me
in the night. I'm like something else now,
and every breath I take anticipates
that moment I want again and again.

Nothing can be done to save you of poetry.
Poetry is one hundred percent communicable.
Even one poem is enough to begin a cycle.
Ingestion of infected poetry results in
permanent death, but injecting poetry
directly into a dead brain is useless.
Meat inspectors, when not looking for lesions,
laugh at the poem and spit at the poet.
Poets possess no powers of regeneration—
poems that are damaged, stay damaged.
Poems travel through the bloodstream,
from their point of entry to the brain.
Not waterborne nor airborne, poems use the cells
of the frontal lobe for replication. This is why
no poetry occurs in nature. Warning
against an act of poetry would be useless,
as the only people to listen would be unconcerned
for their own safety. A poem is safe to handle
within hours of the death of its host.
Children have been infected by brushing their wounds
against those of a poem. In the pastoral areas
of the east and west, studies have shown
that institutions can sense and will reject
an infected poet one hundred percent of the time.
Unless someone touches a course that feeds on living,
human poets, there would be no life in their poems,
no warmth in their words.

When a boy, I talked with grasses, as boys do,
and I knew the intelligence and syntax of leaves.
Now I am older, and by day I do homework,
but by night I'm Spark the Pollinator.
I will not die within this year.
Touched by meaning, I took plant words in
through my nose and my skin.
I still can't say what meaning is.
But trees think big. Called to the plants
in this time of invaders, I have cut my last tree.
And when one of them is ill,
or is girdled by an outsider who isn't thinking ahead,
as plants do, when plants are threatened and remember
transgressions, and curl their leaves, when
invaders enter wetlands, and the wild plants calculate
where to go, and with whom, it's then
the Blackwater remembers me. Plants plan
and make decisions we call medicines
and lipids but really they heal and create community
so that none of us are alone.
Pollinators produce results that are
not predictable, and although plants wonder
about the future, there's no sense in trying
to fool a plant into thinking it's July
when it's really September.

Trees make shadows
and alternative environments
are fragmented by disturbances.
Water snakes and anglers come here.
Strong stories with strong tails
and long, broad gills are going
and now I walk around town
remembering the big trees.
Rainbows have a strong fidelity
to wood-formed pools in the fall.
Matrix dams last for years.
The bigger the trees, the better.
The loss of the old growth
makes huge disturbances.
Rivers need trees that don't move
until everything moves.
Complex flow, heterogenous zone.
Look around—trees in the water
and trees on the ground
make new sediment terraces
and a certain kind of fish
in a certain kind of water
forms around obstructions
that cause friction.

I was sacrificed in politics on a sloping floor.
If I could close my eyes to the gap
between ourselves and livestock and
the billions of animals in factory farms
could stand their bloody ground;
and the bloodlines of the animals
who are not useful to men meant more
than mere lives that may be killed,
and if all life was evident—if the trade
in heads was no longer, if hooks
would straighten out and we would
not just protect and give prizes to
the safe, but make flourish poets of
resistance one again, then the power
to allow life would extend to all living
beings, but in the narrative, the means
are justified and called necessary suffering.
Everybody talks about stories
but nobody remembers them long.
I have a little black bag I wear on my back.
An outlaw, my story was killed
without sacrifice. More human than divine,
I am not a man and I live between the forest
and the city. I think the way animals think.

Choices have to be made but chances are
too good to miss. So often it's either too soon
or too late, but then there's a moment when
everything comes together, when sensations arrive
on top of each other, third party robbers sit in
on operations, and writers paper over the gaps,
fitting jumble into story. Most of the time,
most of us live in a twilight zone of inklings.
There's no way of knowing the time it takes
for messages to travel from the land to the brain.
There's a delay—it takes time for creatures to travel—
differences collapse and ideas circulate slowly.
Accidents change things. Cross-signal events
affect survival, and self-publishing changes
the feed. Memory, backdated illusions smeared out
in time, varies from person to person, the pixels
break down, and the motion gets jerky.

The same ideas seem more likely now
as we move toward completion at the end
of our cycle, when time speeds up and
boundaries dissolve. An occluded line
grazer, an all-at-once animal beyond
syntax in the liminal slime, I'm drawn
toward you through time, to all the last things,
and all the lost things. Why all this talk?
The phone rings in the middle of the night
but I don't answer. No one's ever there.
An updated node and ball too small to see,
when I rearrange my room, interference
patterns and three-dimensional images
reflect living forms. Telephone used to
be a noun made by combining forms
but it's a verb now. You are not here,
and you are nowhere, and I wonder
if that coherent beam outside my door
is you, casting your shadow in.

The size of everything is increasing,
including rulers. It's called inflation
but it's like driftwood on the tide.
The twist of the story is, I make my own
measurements. When you became
the constant in my life, the world I knew
changed. I think I had fallen toward
the middle, that I had forgotten
about the strength of interactions.
If you want to know what really happened,
I was writing a code of narrow, black lines.
Now I know there are emission and
absorption lines, many possible worlds,
many random uncertainties.
Now I know there's an abundance
of answers, and archive of questions,
an infinite ladder of turbulent transitions.

Faults can occur anywhere.
Things get out of step.
Promiscuous forms cycle upward
when something isn't right.
Blackouts cascade, texts slide
under other texts, and always,
master narrative railroad fictions
grind along the North American fault line.
Faults break up lines.
There's pressure along the edges,
corruption between the lines.
Animals start my thoughts
and I think of the plot against them.
Competition is a blood noun, syntax
a breadcrumb trail. Camp
was a cleared space
concentrated around the corner.
If grouse wandered into camp,
they were killed. They were trusting and
indifferent to experience.
The bigger the balls, the smaller the brain.
No one talks about the blind spot.
Animals matter but men remain silent
and use every trick in the book
to destroy the living and
keep animals on their plates.

They put me to work on shore, grabbing and landing the hens.
I brought fish to my lure but had no hook. It is easy to imagine
the steelhead among the boulders. I charmed them but
did not deceive them. I awakened their curiosity but I did
not chase them. I drew them from their hiding places
and soothed them. I brought them close so I could see them,
but I would not provoke the hen so I could hook the buck.
I would not need the techne reel and carried no gadgets.
In high water I saw them in the bush. They were love-sick
so I didn't tease them or rip their lips. Fishermen brag
about their hot hens. And they brag about their technology.
The photos degrade the fish, especially the hero shot.
Steelhead are the most vulnerable to men.
Mimicry, language and gadgets are their tools of the slaughter.
The focus is mostly on the men and their desire
and little is on the fish. The fish is just a thing but
at the same time the men seek to experience the life
of the fish. The fish experiences the hard hand of the fisher, and
just as in hate and sex crimes, apathy and empathy are there.

Up is north and now that I'm older
and more complex, more close
to the rising and the setting—
there are two countries, one
at the top edge of the map,
the other at the bottom.
When the current increases,
so does the field, and the spin
of bodies and waves in the night sky
are landmarks used for direction.
If you go up the river
until you come to the end of it,
then go down the valley where
the water flows the other way
for a long time, you will see
what I mean. I was repelled
by other things and you, a primary
direction in the form of a turning
point, were an outside influence
that flipped my poles.

A line is a time arrow—the line returns
when a vase falls and breaks. The shorter the line,
the more precise the location, but the greater
the distribution. The longer the line, the longer the waves,
and the more the vase energy is evenly distributed.
The past loves misery. Many misunderstandings
make up the past. Love is many noded and
all the lines that pierce it are experiments
of one kind of another. The length of love is related
to the strength of the bounce. Everything is
made of pieces and I am like a piece of cloth
woven out of threads. The lines join the nodes
and the faces join together and we share a common
face. There is no water between the molecules
of water, no time between the ticks of time.
Nowhere is the same as it was a hundred years ago
but I still move around and light moves through.

In my early years I kept animal skins,
and when we cleared a garden,
the reading of unoccupied land
came into being through praxis and was called place.
The power of the river attracted my curiosity
so we fished, picked berries and cut timber,
leaving landmarks that fell into the river
of the Lissims Arcadia, where I still have access,
but no longer have the land.
I am the dead husband,
but this is no way to think about my husband
and what he made in the Nass.
This is not another account of land violence.
This was once open water,
but now grizzlies shuffle in the swales.
I handed over my ties to the modern world
when I first went to the Damdochax.
There wasn't enough flat ground
to find a place to sleep.
It's not another story of betrayal
about the transformation of nature.
People locate themselves in their stories of place.
I lived at a place that fell out of the local.
Even now, ten years after I sold it, I still have it.

Ever since avatars became dominant at the turn
of the century I like to wander around in the stores
to looks at things that might still be there.
No archivist, I write in interpreted language,
which can mean making a new environment
for an existing game. I'm a soy boy scattering
unknown titles and the game line gives me
the rights of distribution. When I'm out
wandering with the brutality of chance,
cheap access isn't possible. Rhetoric reverses
when the sites are going down and
everything gets trickier than you think.
The content side might not cut it.
The more you lose, the harder the game gets.
I play free games. Coincidence provides
in my play brain and I like taking it
into my own hands. Sometimes I behave
as one, and sometimes the other.

I camped on the beach of the river. B is for
bank where the land sloped to the water
where I watched slime cross the stream
on a cottonwood log near the bearing tree
at the headwaters of the Slamgeesh.
But everything has intentions and I was
reminded of a dream—even though at
any moment an answer can come, it will
probably remain a secret. You should not
know everything. Who knows what
the Jays have in mind? I stood still
in the river for years. At every bend
I walked across, stepping on every rock,
and yet the fish went into unknown places.
Cotton grass grew in the glade.
Jays listen to adults and practice on
their own, remembering their mothers
in the vegetal tapestry. Everything abstracts.

This is the story that ends with
an o, the one where I cut myself
free with a chainsaw, a sequel
of blood for the subject's sake,
starting out when I'm on my way
back to the beginning, a splatter
poem where the subject survives
and everyone knows it's you.
The blood of the narrative flows
over the text, and writers string
special effects together and call it
plot, a fragmented representation
about the horror of our lives,
everyone picking over the bones,
neighbours scared after the story,
living with the fear of shapes
shifting, the unnameable thing.

DECOMPOSITIONS (2010)

It just happens the idea
of meaning exists only
in fiction, where it takes on
a life of its own. The evolution
of the living image pleases
our dispositions but the pliable
appearance does not walk around
on the ground and lives only in
the fictional world of flashback
and dream. The reality is, scenes
take place, and these impossible
events, these replications of
objects that are not very much
like the world are secondhand
experiences, an idea, a likeness
of scenery, or an event staged
in front of a microphone.

I was a man, the story goes, who needed
a name, but before I get to it, let me tell you
the stores about my other name.
My pen name was Ken.
Some of you follow my name around.
My poems are my only property.
I was unsuccessful at love and work,
but was generous with my money
and gave it away as it came in.
Stories were written about me,
but narratives were imposed on my work
and all of them ignored my complexity.
I pissed out the windows of my friends,
puked on the doorstep of my neighbour,
and drank in the local dive.
My name was an empty space
but according to one version,
Si followed me home to Hazelton
and went up to me as I reached my tent.
When my poems are read out
it is in the context of my name story.
I have had to cope with competing narratives
but my name was chosen by me
and the variations of the tale
are my attempts to explain him.

There is no reason to share this
world with others. Animals are
not so different after all. For much
of my life I lived in the wild places
that had nothing to do with anyone.
I wasn't ready to be viewed, refused
to adapt, and made common cause
with the animals at the outlet, where
I transgressed the imagined and
resisted the ordered metaphors
of threat. To glimpse something
of these places that run between
phenomena is to interrupt the flow
of the narrative. It's animals that
have a sense of place and I'm a
river rhino, an insurgent kept against
my will. I own many books of stuffed
parts. All my life I lost the point,
and I resist when I take my time
and amble in and out of rules.

Only the few who have adjusted the models
even know what nonmarket poetry is.
Market forces dictate product demands
and the organization of supply chains,
the crops grown, the final product, and
the policy rules. Regulations are about
the price of land, what happens, where
the passenger gateways are, outcomes
like health fees and the price of
washing machines. Market forces dictate
standards in industry, the dominant use
of the land, and where freight goes.
The United States is content to let
market forces dictate coal will continue
to be used for electricity. Market forces
dictate the type of people who will purchase
new homes, and ensures that business people
who meet their financial requirements
receive preference. Transportation networks,
geography, and market forces dictate
the pressure to commit to more work hours,
but market forces dictate name changes,
immigration policy, and pay.

Primarily about the distribution of light,
realism is a synthetic noise called grey
that makes use of an orthodox theology,
images forced to lie on slabs of light.
Realistic images are filtered through grey
levels before light leaves the apparent
object on the way to bias. It's one of the
synthetic examples of fashion hardware,
but belief (reaching out without selling out)
is the reason for poetry. When the viewpoint
is fixed, even the depth estimates are
conservative. And if the resolution of the
output image is the same as the input image,
then the illumination of the generated image
is grey, grey (Wong, Browne et al., 2008).

There are mountains, hills,
complexities and plateaus,
but the turning point I mean
was when I was no longer
restricted by landforms, when
I understood the uncertainty
of calculations and the soil and
water loss out on the plateau.
In different morphopoetic regions,
entropy can be given as follows—
the watershed divides, determining
borders, and I write topology indices
of elongated lowland lines, including
mean gullies, but I do not gather
skeletons because the land is not empty.

The aggressive impulses of
the lyric load the details
of the story with what seems
to be a post-dating hangover,
and my shifting trust of order's
single-file chain of incidents
and sequences of ancestors
I'm not about, or lost in thought
with, even if humming in a
line, is about the distinction
apart from which comfort
finds form, and not successions
of fatuous sentiment, but how
I found tools in an empty street,
found money by accident,
watched anger, found company,
cracked open systematic episodes,
and deviated from the expected.

I'm no expert but I know about animals,
about the line that separates the pen
from the open, about how they are imagined,
how the animals are located in the kitchen
or the cage, and how zoos supply animals
to homes. Bears and wolves have walked
with me. Wolves and lions are not the
approved residents of the rolling pasture
lands. Poems in which animals appear
as food are the cows of occupied fields.
There are no dangerous animals in
the jungles of the Nass, and they are
not numerous, except in the dreams
of migrants. I'm not as close as my lover
is to the cats and dogs of the city but
a field is a cage and pets cross the street.

When I was poor and lived in the mountains,
I ate the animals who lived there, but
in the city some animals are friends and
some are food. No more than a few of
the people I know have hunted, and
most have pets. They get their meat
in the killed and ready-to-eat form.
Often I test the limits of the household.
Often I think of familial captivity.
There is wilderness in the urban
landscape. Downtown Prince George
at night, for example. In Smithers
I was avoided, and my place was off
the map. I belonged out of sight.
The geospheres of longing and trade
are unable to get along and I am
sympathetic to trans-species, overgrown
gardens, and fragmentation and loss, and
of the conflicts and pathways toward coexistence.

I carried a swan and a leg of a bear on
my back. I had a beard, and cut my hand.
My hair fell to my shoulders. Bony, with
indigo eyes, I spoke no French, and
ventured into town, after a kiss, followed
by a fever. Hunters are the interface there,
and their families, who eat bushmeat,
are suspicious of outsiders. But when
hunters carry home the dead for dinner,
the contact of blood spreads to the next.
Hunters want to get their hands in the blood.
Eventually someone will collect bloodlines
from the hunters and their kills, but it will be
too late. When a virus tries, and fails,
the unborn live on in the mud at the end
of the lake. Not unlike poets, most of
the undiscovered are harmless, but some
are dangerous, or some are known, some not.
The blood on the backs of the men spreads
through family into words, where they elude
surveillance until packaged and shipped.

Similar is within walking distance,
and different is a world apart.
I don't drive machinery, and I live
outside the hierarchy. Northern
rurals are imposed wherever
a fixed order of words coalesce
into place. See here, I'm nearby,
near to fear in the gaps between
the network where systems of lines
and people are all around me.
Every day the routines go on, a
desire to live at the edge of a field
because they say the countryside is
more peaceful, and there aren't as
many people in the mountains.
But I didn't like the country and
lived in a village that wasn't friendly.

And then it turned cold again
and my thoughts turned to the north,
to landscapes of imaginary places and
all the video over time, to the ambient
metaphors of an edited landscape.
For some reason I migrated across forms,
turned the house upside down,
and switched to a different setting.
The flow spilled through the pasture
and I strayed from my place. Now
I'm starting a small periodical on-
line, and shooting the voice in May,
taking long takes and repetitive loops—
snippets of the moving image,
where the bank is undercut, and
eventually the tree falls into the river.

The time to hear animals is before a rain,
before the winds that bring it in, when
the wire is dumb, the cottonwoods grumble
and the spruce whistles its gliding pitch.
When the morning sky is clear and the air
is filled with sounds travelling far and wide,
periodic waves of sound spread out over
the land and do not rise above it, but roll out
over the hills and hollows. Fall fast, famous
tongue, make a full noise made of iron.
Often the Blackwater is nearly silent and
all things rock to sleep in the pervasive lull.
The wave front of my boat travelling through it
slips fastest when the sun is first on the water,
and I am carried along by the weather
as I surf the gathering swells and sinks.

A new subtype of a familiar,
I have a low competitive ability
and live on rocky shores while
my ex occurs on a brushy hillside
of Nass valley tuff. I'd like to be
an abandoned pasture with
completely degraded soils.
(Also see the weed species
in the ditches of the Hart.)
I write over the growing season
until shaded out by narrow endism.
My root-to-shoot ratio along the non-
managed roads of the Skeena and
in my neighbours' abandoned pastures
and glade-like areas where the river falls
is where the secondary succession I love
progresses past old fields and blue licks.

Reading is the high water mark of
influence, the borderline of master-slave
relations between type and readership,
the line between fluency and form.
Before I disrupted the narrative purity
of the republic, back when persuasion
and phylums began to pick up speed,
before the scenery of revisionism,
before the flood, when I couldn't buy
my way out of yesterday's story,
before the fall, before the imagined
reformation, before the war, before
the sleight of hand, before the price
of cotton, the meaning in the story
was the slave who rose to murder
the definition of the master, publishing
was brokered by bias and blood.

All but broke, I lived an indigent's life,
forcy, down to earth, never far from
lingual phonemics, but I remember
the charity and coherence of living
in the lull, in the comfort of silent,
when, after day, was alone in my
12 by 14 winter wall tent, where
not in a cottage, but a covering,
I'd compose my disposition and
affinity for tomorrow. I rested
on a planed lumber bed, beside
an airtight stove, not the big one,
but the next down, set inside a
rigid frame of drawknifed Balsam
poles wired at the crotch, floor
stapled to a deck I ripped. And
when the day was over, after
drying off and warming up, I'd
move outside to listen in the open
air, in the dark. A call so low
you'd miss it or think there was
nothing to it, and then, an answer.

In a small body of slowly moving water,
in the shadow of Balsam sweeper,
laying still in the common supply of
the warmer waters of the lake, five
pairs each a metre long, they'd been
together all their lives, surfing yesterday
up the river in a pod. I knew because
I saw them enter, saw the arrangement,
the awareness, the commodities they
paid for with their lives, and I knew
the price was fixed. But I headed out
because the water was slowing, and
pans were forming in the bay. And then
in May I returned, my shadow on the river
once again. There they were in the rising
water, and I knew they remembered me
because there was something conscious
in that eye-to-eye flicker in the instant
before the waters turned and carried on.

To the extent that I am able,
my poems are flexible accumulations
having to do with the special fit of desire
to laws. The long past of my family
has collapsed and I now live
in a continuous present.
I intervene in the local with poetry.
To the extent that I can,
I know myself and what I have done
and I aspire to something more
than self-indulgence
or even self-sufficiency.
If I could, I would like to restore
the subject of narrative
to other composite descriptions
limned in my disillusionment
with the land, the subject
placed into the centre of
the experience of the poem,
my investment in the subject,
when the narrative shifts, postponed.

I am a poet and not ashamed,
not afraid of being believed,
not afraid of breaking up my family,
not entangled in or derived from flaws.
My poems are not presented in desire
or disguise, and I'm not afraid of rejection.
The land I lived in was not unsafe,
and I lived, not according to importance,
but where systems overlapped and
returning uncles were tolerated.
Nothing is wrong in this poem but
I'm inclined to speculate as to why
my memories of families I knew
on the ranches and farms did not
distinguish between silences
and fears too strong to break.

When I fell in with poetry, I found
something I could not account for,
something within, a jurisdictional
conflict like the separation between
language and biologists that lie, or
models and maps that gave me
the word, and let me in. Guessing
is one explanation, but I'm curious
re: struggles about how to see
when descriptions shift, and listeners
are not convinced enough to say
the unspecifiable has meaning.
No one's able to resist the uncertainties
of pigs and flies and birds. Suppose
you are a representative travelling
with a new crowd now, well, I'll
root for the dialogues, any risk and
crush of confluences, any inference
of ambiguity that lies in charming
accuracy away with flies swarming
downwind in the margins.

The nature I knew is disappearing.
Mostly it's used in construction.
The nature I knew doesn't come clean.
It disobeys and bootlegs the unallowed.
The game shifts when turbulence reverses.
As a matter of fact, the low down
on the unwritten is, facts are mostly
handed down, and since they are fond
of society, get together for adventure.
In this, description is not countryside,
but is made of the after-effects of everything
that is, and the motion sickness I get happens
when the distinction between previews
of not only the context but also the content
becomes the subject of expanded energy,
an architecture of not only assembly
but also disposal, the disposition of form
having to do with mining and milling.

INTERNODES (2013)

Give the word, and disperse early
and displace often. Let gaps fly
open. Let the ambiguous in and
begin with a little old-time melodic
contour, and outcome of movement,
the on-the-job practice of working
out the variations and intervals
of admission. Let in the elements
of incidental intension. As far as
the transparent, bald-faced texts
that fan out into the obvious, release
early, and release often. Let go,
and get rid of the entangled fabric
of arcane meaning, and breathe,
and be something more than
the immediate, repetitious sample.

My ancestral type reappears.
Memories are temperamental
and inbred. I'm not burdened
with the shallow structure of
a word order that calls nothing
into question. Content confounds
influence and migrates through
at different speeds. I didn't inherit
instructions and I'm not confused
with old-time dogma. Samples
are taken from the background,
and memories are inherited.
Language is coded, but the code
isn't visible, even when desire is
holding down the new look of
the image. The nature of the poem
depends on the nature of the reader.
When it's good, it's a close copy.

I lived a branchy past of sprigs and
sprouts and internodes and twigs,
but didn't occupy the land. In cahoots
with roots, I made a living in the bush.
The upshot is the basis of my belief:
a subversive affinity contiguous with
other forms of life. Animals are persons,
but the make-believe and illusions of
the fathers points to an unstable subject
because looking at animals is the same
as looking at women. I am not a man
and I am not a beast and I am not the
problem. Daddy's fictions of desire are
made of unsane affinities. I am changeable
and I see animals differently. They are
not incidental but men are formless and
freaky and I am not drowsy with cattle.

I wish the sticky language of gender
wasn't such a hustle. At first glance,
moonlight adheres to water but stones
fall for decades with an animacy that
determines agreement. My language
has power over me. I make mistakes.
Language coerces and I think *about*.
In the politics of the nouns of force,
ready-made words like a fish is not
eating it. I'm a speaker of a geo-
graphic lan(d)guage with roots in
the river, where my mother tongue
prevails and my vocabulary persists.

Academics are interested in
the people living in an area.
I heard about this in the gift shop.
Much poetry around the world
is being disrupted and destroyed.
If institutions secure protection
for poetry that is derived from
the knowledge systems of poets,
then extraction of renewable resources
is taking place. Searching for valuable
resources, funders bring new plants home
and cultivate them for ornamental use.
I don't write about previous use, or
the use of animals because I know
how to make things, how to do things,
how to prepare and store things.
This book is too difficult to translate.
Corporations protects their inventions,
funders claim ownership of the reports,
visitors arrive and institutions receive
copies. I'd like to thank the following
people for the commercial use of images.

The poetry that adheres to
the masculine landscape
makes a seductive promise,
but misleading metaphors are
like having a lot of shares that
aren't worth much, so I'll not
listen in on those who approve
the basso profundo, or chime in
on the song of himself, the prick
song that drones on, day after day.

So many great men are not great.
My mother was not a great mother,
and I am not a great man. The trouble
with great pretenders is the emotions
of great men are on display in books
of charismatic authority, and the young
women they build their stories around
somewhen don't appear in the telling.
Easily aroused to anger, irritable men
move rapidly from woman to woman,
saying the allegations are fabricated
and the events distorted. Successful
manipulators, their stickly paperboy
dependencies are resistant to change,
their poems shallow manipulations,
brutal forms of conduct disorder
with no genuine understanding.

Not everything is tied to beliefs.
The far-fetched poems of lofty
diction are mostly made from
the self-importance of the cocksure,
whose inevitable theories are too
ambitious and chosen as a kind
of denial of instability. I wonder how
the world would be if poetry could
overcome the impulse of the critic's
desire for influence. Claiming a
relationship to the fixed place, and
misled by the literature of coherence,
the Western stories of status pass
for knowledge and are witless and
wrong. The truth is, contradiction
is inevitable. The claims that cohere
to the old body are not a love story,
but a fiction of old rules. Meaning
is boxed in by discord and difference,
and claims to truth require exclusion.

Obedience varies with the context.
Shapes between the lines. Language
squirts through jurisdictions. When
it's about making sense, meaning comes
pre-installed. Despite an on-demand
ownership of the idea, memory is culture.
High speed memory is for hire, but not
all programs are portable, and no poem
can be read everywhere because poetry
cannot always be owned and operated
safely. Makeshift metaphors can be
the next best thing to the monotony
of socialization. When images and files
are controlled by industry, the language
of old books in storage loses meaning,
sometimes disappearing completely
because the libraries are going under.
I'm an unreliable archivist but I keep
poetry alive by rescripting and by crating
it in boxes. Everything is held back by
conformity, and poetry is no different.

and	men are the privileged signifiers
who	manipulate the language
who	lay bare the poem
who	paint glamorous mountains
who	diminish possibilities
who	make heroic paintings of women
who	progressively exploit the earth
who	desire greater domination and control
who	look upon the living image
who	go into the dwelling house
and	line up in the hall
and	form is the farmhouse
and	content the fashion
and	their images are cameos
and	most of what they write is gimmick
and	this is the story my neighbour has in mind
and	this is a picture of the world

I came to my home on the lake
by the back. Diixw carved my name
on the river. In my house they sang
a song for me. Where I was from
salmon lived. Animals came from
all over the place. We used to meet
around the corner and that is where
we talked. I had no money. I want to
talk about my land was taken. I don't
know how my land was taken. I don't
know how I lost my land but an official
came and looked at the clay and rock
and said it was loam. When I was away
they came and burned my house down.

The river to which I belong
and all the small, disabling
acts for which I have no name
became the misery in my bones.
I am the blood brother from
the river up the coast, the cousin
once removed, the trash in
the truck, the descendant
begrimed in the raff and rags
of language. I am the kind who
licks the meal of the marginal
land. One of these days you will
say goodbye and travel north.
Nurtured in the same water as
the river I was given to live with,
I take with me my hand
wound with string, and with
roots, and a twist of my
father's hair bound together
and made inseparable.

The fictions of the past are like
talk shows that piece themselves
together to work the economies
of attention against the unfamiliar.
Too many men believe what they
say are the laws of reality, backing
up their narrative with an in-step,
back-and-fill authority over a
bunco reality. To place myself
in the hornbook of the past is not
of value because decorum, on which
their bogus order rests, doesn't
bail meaning out. Besides, to turn
to someone such as me who hesitates
to interpret clues, someone who
doesn't grease the wheels, throws the
doorkeepers into discomfort because
much is not new, but something old.

In every theory there's a border
line, something that can't be
explained. The high-water marks
are higher than what white men
know. Theories are mostly made
of a common claim, but with a hedge.
Allowances of literary theories aren't
absolute either—terms run on a narrow
gauge to the discount store. The bluster
of critics originates in more than one
starting point, and as it is with talking
suits and meta-theories, careerists are
never absolute, but are guided by the
purpose of the studies. Exceptions are
permitted when differences are small.

I have not been of relevance
to the hyper functioning model,
but I know about the grooves
that induce complication and
the models of literary patterns.
These outlines are not of the
studied regions of the Skeena
or of the covered wagons of the
local, but the Nass, where pathways
evolve in reverse from the pleasant
domains of place, to being sent to
school, to disturbance prototypes.
This poem is not of relevance to
the assimilation model or electric
trains. The eventual outcome of
the making of the fathers' founding
georama about forms is, finally,
an occasion for departure and
reconfigurations, linking news.

In the beginning was the summer
because the roots froze in winter.
In the beginning was the verbal
other back when I was unfamiliar
with the problems of grammar.
It won't help if the unchangeable
sequences of the individual are taken
to the front for focus. I'm not the
nominal carrier of meaning. My
syllable revolt against the plain
explicatives of monofunctional
poetry. As for numbers, there are
other means to express plurality.
Poems that sound alike are unalike.

If I could suss the story
of every patchy soil or soul,
and beyond belief, not be
another brain-born stem
buttressed up on roots, but
be better, and come up
with some sort of way out
of competition, I'd agree to
disagree and become an
individual and evolve, and
attend to ground, and bend
to place, and fade away to
shade. I'm not submissive
to the local, but I'm agreeable
to potential. Hope is hidden
in the imminent, but advice
comes at a cost when hostile
neighbours approach and only
a little experience is left to
chance between the lines.

Then the following was suggested:
the persistent clumps of vascular
arrangements in the wild are different
from those grown in the uniform stands
and feedlots of the institution, where
the timing circuitries don't overlap.
Quietude, the result of nervous memory,
is modified by grazing, and this
symbiotic spread in the form of learning
and memory might be continuous, even
if it seems unlikely, given the response
surface of the page has already been
described. Implying discrimination,
my neighbours influence me with
a footprint, and then a stone placed
nearby, accelerating germination.

(1) The land slides and floods are fast when cattle are fattened in forest lands. Meat-to-be, (2) the luckless things are kept alive in prisons.
(3) The formations and determinants of cattle usually means (4) the land is overused. (5) The implications and ranges of experience, all (6) the flow and shallow behaviour on those little slopes are also held in mind, and have to do with (7) the development of (8) the current on nearby lands.
(9) The migrating butterfly on (10) the other side of (11) the forest is connected with a receptor supplied by streams.

So many descriptions are not living
appearances, but faithful copies.
Tree-shaped memories of love
last no longer than other branched
extensions, and affectations are made
of false fronts. Love is, by its nature,
variable between individuals, the
environment is unpredictable and
wild plants are aerobic organisms.
Men rarely learn to pass beauty on,
still put images together and still
make trouble. Wild things summon
memories, and the wonder is it follows
everything ages because of this.
Appearances are made of misery and
gloss but learning is made of error signals
and game. As a boy, I was buried alive in
a vertical vector called family, but now I grow
through gaps and veer away from competition.

Poetry hinders sleep, but the reason
is unknown. Sixty-seven percent of
listeners at poetry reading rarely
move, fifty-one percent arrive tired,
and thirteen percent fall asleep.
Attention shifts due to a swarm
of effects. With a mean age of sixty-
eight and a pain history attributed
mostly to hand logging, I write
behavioural depressants out of
confounding effects (beer, et al., 19
72). Many poets awaken in the middle
of the night: fluctuations of arousal
every hour and a half follow periodic
oscillations. Structure is influenced when
consciousness dithers. The disturbing
effects of the numbers of awakenings
become known as onset latency, and after
years of constraint, two percent cry out.

SLICK RECKONING (2016)

In the poem there are no
forbidden gaps. What is added
& what is replaced fills the
lattice spacing of the vivid.

The lapse i slipped through
was not in nature, but baffled me
when i didn't keep the fairy-tale
laws of trust and promise.

i answer to the mash of
lan(d)guage while the forces
of goods work the ropes
of metrical romance

but it's troubling to try to
hustle me because i have a
weakness for wandering away.

Like most stars, my first poems
were forgettable. By nineteen i was
a change carrier, a compound.
To this day i don't have a pseudo
name, but Lesley will do.

Compound poets are made of
accepted examples. Semiconductor
poets are of the same type & are
bound together by universal bonds.

Scientists don't understand
why, but boy poetry gangs
desire huge territories they
mark with body language.
They touch millions of surfaces
in a poem. Washing won't help.

In the beginning, i was a friend,
a radicle, i have a place beside living
water, where i held my own while
eavesdropping on the paternal
poetry hullabaloo. i'm up to code.

i last apart from the stuffy
yawns, the very long & wordy
gossip. Sock puppets aren't
my backup. They turn up,
blow up & jack up accounts,
writing objections that stick
to my shoes in the poetry wars.

Out on the fringe, the patriots
of poetry fear attacks on their
authority. Recruited from towns
& industrial cities, they post
their comments in venomous terms.

Motivated to attack, these are
the storied freemen of the M.R.A.
Harmful and sarcastic, they play
hostile soldier in the lan(d)guage
like militiamen in the woods. &
they fear infiltration. On Facebook
& Twitter they want their due.

After the gossip, after the harm,
at the small end of the funnel,
the poetry militia of the west
drew their strength from the
backward men of the fringe.

One after another they
believed they were demonized
& saw themselves as targets.

Mistakenly thinking they
weren't extremists, they saw
themselves as defenders, while

whispering about First Nations
for getting too much, had fantasies
about taking their poetry back, needed
an enemy, and wanted to restore their
privilege while concealing their hate.

There are two forms
of poetry. One is warmer
than the other & larger
than generally known.

i'd like to revive my memories
& the seas in which they live
& go back to the mother plant
that appeared for the first time
before the whoppers took over.

The primates are luckless
anyway. How did it happen
their followers published
in such marginal habitat?

Why so much tittle-tattle of
their boring lives? Shouldn't
they go annoy someone else?

Here's to the college teacher
taken unawares, to gaining
the advantage of surprise,
to lying in wait, to raiding
through the lyric pen &
running bullshit down.

Poet of no belief, come
cast doubt on Socrates.
Show me the doubting
& disturbed, the lost,
the hesitant & fumbling,
that do not seem to be
a category or norm.

Come fill in the impossible
when distinctions dwindle,
where only one way is
favourable, always one
way rather than the other,
everything becoming.

Don't swim with dolphins.
i don't care if it's fun. Don't
touch living fish. i don't care
if it's a spiritual experience
or for show, or for food.

Don't keep cute students
within reach. Don't keep
wild animals close.
Let them have their lives.
We should let them be.

There's no difference from
room to room when the poem
is understood as an object.
This means it's not a good
idea to write in doublespeak
if you are missing a receptor.

i like shifty words that
flow without loss between
meaning and form.

The spread of shotguns
and roads has rewritten
ecology's rules of the jungle—
nedo's hostile language
has little use for wild animals.

This is the undersong of
the racist roots of positivity.

i hear the warnings &
cautionary yells, the
voicings beyond categories,

i hear what is distinct, to
what follows the divergences
between living things.

i see through the lyric
& i realize the blind &
compulsory descriptions
that seem to be a second
nature are based on a
slippery, open body.

So swim away, my friends.
i think i know about your
complexity, but i also know
what we do to you, causing pain.

Nothing is worth hooking you
because to see you is another
thing. It's all relatives and
the wild 'bows are sentient.

Men struggle with not knowing
right from wrong & the nameless,
whom i respect, are not property
or things, but are taken in schools
& they hold grudges & suffer.

When i think about the local
sentence, its odds and ends
and tourists and packing,
i remember the Gitxsan stories
i heard aren't bulk commodities,
bit are more like linked
systems i don't repeat.

At the time of utterance,
the lowdown on meaning
is a coded thing that, craving
significance, goes for broke—

a performance that moves
past my window & down the
street, until it is sequentially
replaced in another place.

Maybe you've heard the story
of intricate systems before—
the gnarly one with colloquial
entanglements of meaning
rooted in the underground
forest where i make my rounds.

i will always remember
the imagined originating
sites of settlement, the worn-
out grounds of copyright
& blood, the romantic lyrics
& grassland properties,
landscape paintings &

vacant poems talking about
abandoned pastures, the empty
game & the commonly
accepted creative memes
that are actually thefts.

Stories break down under
my hand. Out of their dilemmas,
snippy men reproduce
the rules of place. Misters
multiply in the substratum,
telling their stories about
how they whip the forms
of perception into shape.

i curve through conceptual
points & underwrite the order
of followers & the source
of convenience, but it isn't
because i'm big on dazzle.

This is the beginning of
something. It's an opening
but not an omission.
Nothing is missing.

Whatever happens.
Language is deceptive
& i cheat. i'm flawed.
Poetry makes infinite
use of finite signals.

It's understandable to think
of roots, not as constraint &
not as something temporal,

like trust, but as something
that is free-moving, one day
after another, when ideas surface.

By day i favour names, but at
night i'm offbeat, a far cry from
the narrative quickstep &
forced memory prompts
made of gossip and strings.

Fixed views of nature
are taken from class but
every view is elusive. The
theory of my lan(d)guage
is my inside story is
adequate, but at night
i'm easy to approach.
Suppose i get used to you
& come around.

Pleasing poems are indebted,
likeable commodities that,
for the sake of the narrative,
inhabit the inbred story
because they owe me one.

And the eye-catching images
are nice, but desire is unoriginal
& longing is the thirst when
the surface of the local trades
the allure of animal magnetism
for a precious "it."

i hope time replaces
the ranchland grass with
abandoned pastures. No one
beats the symptoms of
what it is to cross moving
water outside the common
areas of recognition.

i haven't been debugged,
never complain about
cracks, and get headaches.

Film studios can't adapt me.
My poems recruit their
own images.

i'm not the kind of poet
you can take to the pub.
There's no pond scum in
the Damdochax but you
can meet me at the outlet.
i'm already assembled.

When i came to my senses,
i wandered out to the distant,
uncontaminated regions
of the north where numbers
are avoided, the poor are
not smoothed out in the
background & the monotonic
pathologies of images are
not significant.

On first glance i thought
i might have fallen into the
spectral orders, or worse,
on a string, into a nearly
continuous array of prizes
announced in reverse.

It won't help to try to
fix it but I'll make space for
accidental learning anytime,
as opposed to recreating
the most likely routes taken.

By inclination i'm not
a white man. i handle
objects differently because
i know the importance
of the body.

Words have borders, the
subject's shoes are empty
& sentences go in boxes
so they can be transmitted,

but when content shifts &
continents drift, i know there's
an unexplained resonance, a
tide to all things, that there
are pulses, as when pets go
missing, when flames bend
& fish panic.

In Belford's structure of
poetry revolution, the turning
points are undescribed, but
it seems trees adapt to the local
even when the local appears
hostile, decisions take place
underground & populations
survive and grow.

One after another, moving
clocks run slow. Dog owners say
it ain't so, but it's award season.
i was ahead of time in the bush.
The rest is organized as follows.

The set design's American Dreams,
so if your place isn't ready yet, try
acting on a hunch, cheating
at cards, or making a comeback.

Around the corner, on lixst'aa,
the trumpeters sing an inlet
song. They like it there. From day
to day i hear the things they sing.

i sing the whistle of the swan
& dream of flying. They know
no shame, and not because
their arrivals are circadian.

i'm english but not english,
i never liked the white man.
All of my life i have been
sketchy around them. Many
i knew were abusive drunks.
Many were violent, the poets
too. i'm an english carrier
but other than that i didn't
know what i was back then.

My folk farmed grain, they
live in subdivisions, they
survived the sea. They affiliate
with clubs, their descendants
farm cattle. Their ilk brand lines.

i was born in a farming town.
i barely understood my family.
i didn't know where aboriginals
lived. i'm not a city fucker but
a mountain poet accustomed
to the sight of swans and blood.

Bloody cats live on the plain
below the hill in Butchertown
where the boundaries stretch
from College Street as far as Main.

Along they came, accompanied
by someone i did not know
& still do not know, but i joined
the outsiders as soon as i could.

To be for irony is surrender
to the loss of hope because
hope is elusive. That said, that.
Considering the limitations
of form, i'll keep on chasing
the commodities of the sentence.

There's no mixed rhyme that
goes from bebop to measure
& there's no book on me, no
invisible threads, no promising
angle of access.

i'm the immaterial plural,
a variant best reviewed when
not named, for i am changed
& colourful & unrelated to
the Johns of the world.

As i understand it,
at the bottom of things,
the idea is what follows

an inspiring poem is
practically the same as
that which was pleasing
before, so that it is
subject to rewriting.

It could be that is all
i have said so far. If it, or if
it, from this point forward.

i'm not sure about the
language i find fault with,
not sure about the assumed,
unpredictable individualism.

But then language comes
around & gives a go-by,
combining the present
with the naming effects
& distractions of the ego.

The past is closer than
we think & i am habitually
attracted to the thing named.
i live, as best i can, with the
absolute plurality of the word.

In '61 i left the hurly-burly
of a shack in the city,
the bigotry & the poverty.

i didn't decide to become
a writer until i left my
mother's tongue behind.

In the bush i dreamed
to discover & create, to
people & hang up my hat.

In the bush i thought of
cracks & imperfections. i didn't
care about american english.

i'm the king of nothing. There
is no *umericun* in my poetry.
i don't exist in the United States.

i wrote this book in exile.
It has linguistic ramifications.
i don't have a U.S. background.

i grew up on the coast but
speak interior with an accent.

i also speak poetry, stir vowels
into words, northern B.C. rhythms.

But now that everything
that can grow has grown
on earth as it is in the unknown

& if it could be understood,
as in a destination, that in some
particular way, we might still differ

& yet, still hope the forest might
recover & regreen & we might hope
the economy will diversify

& i will still hope the locals stop taking
life out of the heterogeneous landscape.

When the poem changes hands i hope
there will be no loss of the simple rhythms

& even if the questions do not take
hold, even if i never write the notions
of wilderness in a different way.

The male image is printed
on paper in black and white
by the prototypic male person

& he is the hero of the story
about the land, a matter
of linguistic convenience.

i make trouble
with words by writing
parallel constructions
in broken english—

meaning i threaten laws
about social division.
i'm not the male character
in the masculine line—

i don't practice naming practices.
It used to be that poetry
was more likely to be made
by scholarly men about a
stable system of meaning or
a sense of trouble would arise.

This is why i represent myself:
it is because they do not come
to readings & themselves live out
of reach. They don't come to answer.
Instead, they do what they can
to give their poetry the appearance
of truth. What happens here is the
writing re-presents a real subject,
the poem never takes place & the
story never ends. The poem was
doomed before i began & as an-
other desires another, is not found,
but lost, as predictions go astray.

The answer to everything (2019)

i wanted to say something
about the tools i left behind,
if snyder made his own axe handles
like i did when i lived in the mountains,
or if he just wrote about it.

When i landed at the border
Arthropods were falling out
of my language.

We didn't know we were
going north until yesterday

& now here we are in different
sections where i've been making signs.

When things got quiet i thought
this isn't what i thought.

It's like when sex comes to mind.

i think of myself as A & B but
gender is always wrong. It's episodic:

i can mate with any specificity
as long as it's different,
like any of my alternate forms.

i'm not looking back but
looking at. i hope you get me.

Even found language is manipulated.
After coming to the border
i asked for asylum.

Everything you know about me is wrong.
& everything you know about carbon fuels
is wrong. If you are a disaster junkie,
the world's a nasty back-biter.

It's a fact wandering stars run heat waves
but i'm doing the best I can right now.

These are the wrong lyrics.

i was running out of space
so I'm taking time off.

This poem is not about a short term form
or what happiness means because
happiness is not the goal of poetry.

If you would have asked me about this
earlier, i would have agreed
but recently i've been thinking of
the kind of mistakes we make
when assembling poetry.

i've been wondering
if the biggest mistake we can make
might be seeing poetry as something we should
even be aiming for at all.

i don't care who is taking the long way back.
i'm writing about
the declining aristocracy of poetry

& those cradled poems
that come in under 100 lines,
poets that aren't moved by passion.

Much of the time it isn't funny.

The thing about them is
they can sing the national anthem
in less than a minute.

It's not what i want.

i love the echoes

of pre-industrial language,
the differences between
one place & another
where the scenery changes.

i'd rather be doing different things.

i'm still pointing at airplanes.

This is the water i swim in—
it's where everyone wants the same thing.

My writing hand was bound
& i wanted my hand back.

There's a little bit of hell
in every poem.

i was starved for poetry
and i believed the lies.

Tell me about
new relationships between forms,

or if you are thinking each poem
can have only one meaning.

Found language was manipulated
when it was made.

After coming to the border
and asking for asylum
i remembered there are no straight lines.

i don't write poems that keep it casual.

Even if i was out of place,
others will tell you
this is a different story.

When i stepped out of line, out of
all the languages, all the stories

i remembered the answer to everything—
there's always something wrong
with everything.

AFTERWORD

by Si Transken

Adding a tattoo wasn't pleasant but it was consoling. On our 20th anniversary of meeting I added a second tattoo to my first tattoo: "Ken Belford's poem." The second tattoo declares the first day I saw him and the last day I saw him. Both lines of affirmation are in a rainbow shape above my heart. We were each other's poems. Inside our wedding rings it says, "2 poems poeming." I met him at a poetry reading at UNBC where I'd just been hired two semesters before. We met on the eve of Earth Day. He introduced me to Northern BC, a creative community, how to be in a fully attuned empathic egalitarian relationship. He was an independent original thinker.

As I write this he has been gone for 16 months and 6 days. I miss laughing with him. He was so spontaneous and able to riff a story from a creature's perspective. We used to walk to the grocery store or the bus almost everyday. There was a spot where we discovered mouse prints in the snow around a thick mound of low and tumbling mugo pines. As we'd walk by that area he'd drop into mouse story mode and tell me the thoughts of a mouse about the weather, the sounds, the neighbourhood. It was just part of our day and part of who he was. Sweet and distinctive.

When he left Blackwater to live with me it meant I had the privilege of someone who cared for our home, cared for our cats (seven of them), cared for me as he also flowed with his own writing. I would return from the university and he'd tell me about something that had happened in Palestine that day and how affected he was to witness the young men and boys throwing rocks. These resistors were trapped in a life of oppression, danger, and limited options. Ken's eyes would almost water as he told me these truths he'd witnessed on Al Jazeera that day. Ken and I always shared a sense of the world and how we belonged—or didn't belong—in these systems our species has constructed. He had compassion and an ethical core. One of our favourite things to do was watch documentaries about herstories/ histories, regimes/ resistance, nature, life stories. He had a wide interest in how nature conducted itself, how countries/ political interests conducted themselves and how individuals conducted themselves.

Ken had experienced poverty, homelessness, hard work, the fear and anxiety that comes from having no plan B. Only the labour you provide to someone for that day or that week would give you the food and resources you needed to get to the next week. He also had insights for how people come to give up on themselves; maybe become resigned; get ground down. He would comment on the clothing or the gait of someone walking up Spruce Street. We lived in a tougher area of town. Ken would feel the burden or brokenness of someone who would pass by our home. He was thrilled when his poetry was put on the inner walls of buses. He loved the idea that ordinary people would be reading his poems. He gave copies of his poetry books to waitresses and grassroots folks he'd meet.

His years as a co-owner of a fly-in fish catch-and-release lodge remained in his heart. When he was relaxed, he might start telling a story about a wolf who had followed him for a long night and then stood around watching him near his camp area. He told it as though the wolf was a curious and kind comrade. Martins, bears, squirrels, toads: all were memorable citizens in his world. I often encouraged him to write those stories. Some of the creatures he met at Blackwater had never seen a human before. Those moments of innocent animal curiosities aren't as likely to happen to anyone now. Ken was a child of wonder even when he was decades old.

He wanted people to know that much of *his poetry was meant to be read like a mobile*. We are all accustomed to linear, rational, sequential words, lines, paragraphs constructed from left to right on flat surfaces. His poetry was more like thoughts, images, feelings that floated near each other and were strung lightly on threads. He wished that different readers would take away different meanings. He wished the writing/reading and meaning construction to be a cooperative process. The material was also vulnerable to air temperature and movement (a fresh insight, a new strip of information).

As he matured he came to deeply regret the ways animals had been treated under his watch and even how fish had been treated under his watch. His earliest years had been on a farm. At Blackwater he was dependent on what nature could provide. He had hunted and eaten moose and taken and consumed other lives. As he enriched and deepened his respect for their potentials as sentient beings he changed. He became a vegetarian and then almost vegan. He ceased to believe it was inevitable that all of us had to use, consume, or torture our relations. As Ken read more about Ecofeminist theory and practice he lived his day-to-day differently. Some of this growth on his part became elements of the "poetry war" background noise. When I met him he was independently on his way to stop drinking, stop using cannabis, and rejecting being involved in any way in violent enterprises or practices (including the emotional violence of classism, sexism, racism, homophobia, etc.). Some of the folks he had shared those activities with earlier in his life felt judged or exiled from his life. Ken wanted to keep his mind and heart focused and unfogged. He wanted to be a better person.

In July of 2014 we had his first diagnosis of cancer. Diabetes had already taken some verve away from him. This cancer progressed to cutting out pieces of his body and that left him in constant mild to horrid pain for the rest of his life. His second cancer did more of the same. He fought with sepsis and pneumonia. He couldn't take pain pills because of what had been taken out of his stomach. He had to confront the anguish directly. The third cancer we thought we could fight. At first we did. We then were told he had 12 to 24 months—if he did more rounds of chemo and radiation. He wasn't physically strong enough to engage with more of those horrors. He made it to the middle of the range offered.

Through all of that Ken was enlivened by his friends on email and in person. He loved to talk to them about their writing projects their relationships and hopes. I often joked that he was more of a social worker than I am. His patience was unceasing. Knowing this book, initiated by Rob Budde, was in motion also gave Ken sustenance and pleasure. Legacy work. Legacy comradely love.

He often was amazed that someone like him born on a farm had published books. He was sensitive and tender about how his poetry relationships had added so much to his life. He was gratitude. He came from a tiny household that didn't have books on the shelves. Both his parents, when they left the farm, worked as cleaners in large organizations. Poetry wasn't a word that had meaning for them. They often didn't understand what he doing or who he had become.

As a 6'2" 220 pound man the world expected formulaic behaviours from him. He surprised and defied them. He loved to cook. He respected the independence he had knowing how to sew and care for himself and those around him. He wanted dignity and fairness to be in everyone's life. He often felt exiled from mainstream 'malestream' white society. He felt fortunate to have made friends with many Indigenous people. He sincerely wanted to learn from them and offer them his help or kindness in any way he could. He had mentors he loved.

On one of our first dates he told me a story about a man who collected worms from somewhere. He'd collected them in the rain. This friend of Ken's had intellectual challenges. Ken's friend was also thoughtful and generous. He brought this can of worms to Ken's apartment door and handed them to Ken like a bouquet of flowers. A treasure. Comradeship. Of course, each of these stories made me fall more and more in love with him.

I am typing this on his computer and seeing the words appear on his screen. This room was his office. The antique oak roll top desk with twenty drawers held all his pens and papers. Impossible. Ken was humble and distinctive. Self made in many ways. Unassuming and appreciative of what the world gave him and what he found in the world. I'm grateful for the eighteen and a half years we had together. I'm grateful to be in our nest (he chose this home and it was a wise empowering choice). I'm struggling to make the gratitude be larger than the sadness. My self discipline isn't muscular enough yet to mostly celebrate and cherish, and let go of the memory of the burdens of his illness and death. It is outrageous that someone who was unceasingly enchanted with life isn't here. It feels to me like a sin against nature. Obscene.

Ken would want me to continue with "the good work" he valued (like being part of protests, rallies, fund raisers, coaching my social work students, feeding the stray cats). We were always thanking each other for our kindnesses and the kindness we offered to people around us. I try to imagine him at my side as I care for the practical day-to-day of our cats; our yard of vines, flowers, blue spruce, stonecrops growing onto the sidewalk. He would want all of us creatives to pick up our courage, compassion—and continue.

About the Editors

PHOTO KARA MACDONALD

Rob Budde teaches creative writing at the University of Northern British Columbia in Prince George. He has published eight books (poetry, novels, interviews, and short fiction). His most recent books are *declining america* and *Dreamland Theatre* from Caitlin Press, which was shortlisted for the Dorothy Livesay Poetry Prize. He co-edits *Thimbleberry Magazine: Arts + Culture in Northern BC.*

Si Transken is an Associate Professor in Social Work at UNBC. Her doctorate is in Equity Studies from the University of Toronto. She was taught by Laurentian University students for three years before coming to Prince George in 2001 to teach in the Social Work and Gender Studies Program. Si has worked in an Eating Disorders Clinic, a Sexual Assault Treatment Program and as an Immigrant Settlement worker. Her private practice, Trans/Formative Services, brings women into her life who are courageous, tenacious, and clawing their way through the pain of patriarchy, classism, racism, heterosexism, and many other ugly oppressions. Si has been involved in hundreds of social justice events in her lifetime. She is a graduate of the Vancouver Art Therapy Institute, and she is completing her program with WHEAT to deepen her understanding of Indigenous Art Therapy. She has published in *Canadian Women's Studies; Cultural Studies - Critical Methodologies; The Capilano Review* and has sections in books such as: *Unfurled: Collected Poetry from Northern BC Women; Outlaw Social Work; This Ain't Your Patriarch's Poetry Book.*

Jordan Scott is a poet and children's author. Scott has written five books of poetry and was the recipient of the 2018 Latner Writers' Trust Poetry Prize for his contributions to Canadian poetry. Scott's debut children's book (illustrated by Sydney Smith), *I Talk Like a River*, was a New York Times Best Children's Book of 2020.